What's on the Food Chain Menu?

by Julie K. Lundgren

Science Content Editor:
Kristi Lew

www.rourkepublishing.com

Science content editor: Kristi Lew
A former high school teacher with a background in biochemistry and more than 10 years of experience in cytogenetic laboratories, Kristi Lew specializes in taking complex scientific information and making it fun and interesting for scientists and non-scientists alike. She is the author of more than 20 science books for children and teachers.

www.rourkepublishing.com

Project Assistance: The author wishes to thank Amber Burnett for her expert information on gray jays.

Photo credits: Cover © Magdalena Bujak, kontur-vid, S1001, Cover logo frog © Eric Pohl, test tube © Sergey Lazarev; Table of Contents © Jens61er; Page 4/5 © Steve Byland; Page 6 © Margaret M Stewart; Page 7 © jennifer leigh selig; Page 8 © (see cover) PILart; Page 9 © Rusty Dodson; Page 10 © PILart; Page 11 © Ozerov Alexander; Page 13 © Gerrit_de_Vries, Oleg Znamenskiy, Andrejs Jegorovos; Page 14 © Jens61er, Wolfe Larry, Vasyl Helevachuk, PILart; Page 15 © Arthur van der Kooij; Page 16 © NOAA; Page 17 © Cindy Haggerty, Andrea Leone, Vebjorn; Page 18/19 © Mauro Rodrigues; Page 20 © vitek12; Page 21 © Tom Mc Nemar

Editor: Kelli Hicks

My Science Library series produced for Rourke by Blue Door Publishing, Florida

Library of Congress Cataloging-in-Publication Data

Lundgren, Julie K.
 What's on the food chain menu? / Julie K. Lundgren.
    p. cm. -- (My science library)
 Includes bibliographical references and index.
 ISBN 978-1-61741-745-0 (Hard cover) (alk. paper)
 ISBN 978-1-61741-947-8 (Soft cover)
 1. Food chains (Ecology)--Juvenile literature. I. Title.
 QH541.14.L865 2012
 577'.16--dc22
                              2011004758

Rourke Publishing
Printed in the United States of America,
North Mankato, Minnesota
060711
060711CL

www.rourkepublishing.com - rourke@rourkepublishing.com
Post Office Box 643328 Vero Beach, Florida 32964

Table of Contents

Animal Needs

The place an animal lives is its habitat. Habitats contain everything an animal needs to survive.

Eastern bluebirds find tasty insects, grubs, and berries to eat in their woodland habitat.

Animals need water, **nutrients**, and safe resting places. They find these **nonliving** things in their habitat. Animals use the habitat's living things for food.

A chipmunk rests in its burrow.

A thirsty moose and her calf drink water.

Chain of Life

Plants grow. Some animals eat plants. Some animals eat the plant eaters. A food chain links living things.

Mice eat grain. Milk snakes eat mice.

Green plants are **producers**. They use the Sun's energy, water, and air to make food for themselves. Plants begin food chains.

Plants need the Sun's energy to make food.

Consumers eat other living things. **Herbivores** eat plants. **Carnivores** eat other animals.

Prepare to Lunch:
ON SAFARI

What's on the menu in the African grasslands? Herds of herbivores, such as wildebeests and zebras, eat different types of leaves and grasses.

The herbivores become meals for carnivores like lions and cheetahs.

Omnivores are consumers, too. They eat both plants and animals.

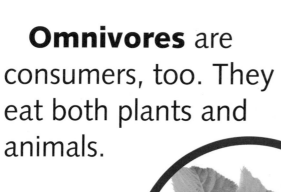

Red foxes are omnivores. They eat fruit, mice, insects, frogs, and rabbits.

15

Predator is another name for a carnivore. Predators hunt and eat **prey**. Fish, seals, and polar bears are all predators in the Arctic.

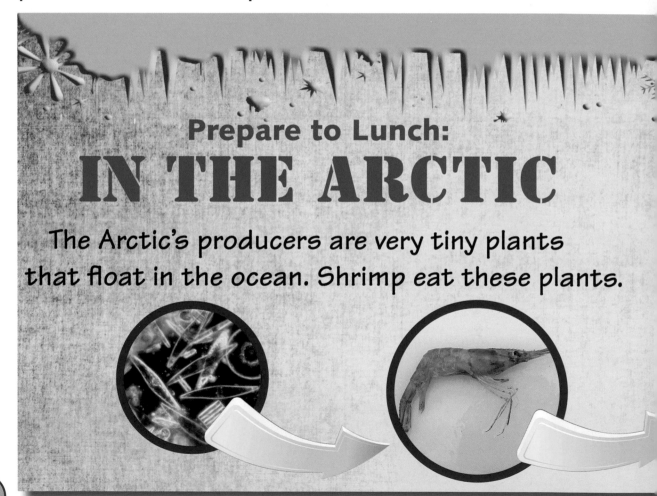

Prepare to Lunch:

IN THE ARCTIC

The Arctic's producers are very tiny plants that float in the ocean. Shrimp eat these plants.

Then fish eat the shrimp and seals eat the fish. Polar bears eat the seals.

Finally, A Fresh Start

When plants and animals die, their bodies break down with the help of **decomposers**, such as **bacteria** and mold. Animals like earthworms and sowbugs also help break down dead plants and animals.

Sowbugs munch on rotting plants.

Decomposers turn nature's waste into soil nutrients. Plants use these nutrients to help them grow. Plants can begin the food chain again.

Mushrooms, a type of decomposer, recycle nutrients for new life.

21

SHOW What You Know

1. What things do animals need in their habitat?

2. Can you give an example of a food chain?

3. What would Earth be like without decomposers?

Glossary

bacteria (bak-TEER-ee-uh): common microscopic living things that act as decomposers

carnivores (KAR-nuh-vorz): animals that eat other animals

consumers (kahn-SOO-merz): living things that cannot produce their own food

decomposers (dee-cum-POH-zerz): tiny living things that cause rot and decay

herbivores (HUR-buh-vorz): animals that eat plants and not other animals

nonliving (non-LIV-ing): without life

nutrients (NEW-tree-uhnts): things needed for healthy growth, like vitamins and minerals

omnivores (AHM-nih-vorz): animals that eat both plants and animals

prey (PRAY): an animal hunted by predators

producers (proh-DOO-serz): plants that use energy from the Sun to make their own food

Index

Websites

www.animalfactguide.com/

www.ecokids.ca/pub/eco_info/topics/climate/adaptations/index.cfm

www.litzsinger.org/weblog/archives/2005/10/the_hidden_life.html

www.uen.org/utahlink/activities/view_activity.cgi?activity_id=4750

About the Author

Julie K. Lundgren grew up near Lake Superior where she liked to muck about in the woods, pick berries, and expand her rock collection. Her interests led her to a degree in biology. She lives in Minnesota with her family.